THE MONSTER IN ME

By Hunter & Darin Bullivant

AuthorHouse™
1663 Liberty Drive
Bloomington, IN 47403
www.authorhouse.com
Phone: 1-800-839-8640

First published by AuthorHouse 06/28/2011

ISBN: 978-1-4634-1109-1

Library of Congress Control Number: 2011908540

Printed in the United States of America

Any people depicted in stock imagery provided by Thinkstock are models,
and such images are being used for illustrative purposes only.
Certain stock imagery © Thinkstock.

This book is printed on acid-free paper.

Because of the dynamic nature of the Internet, any web addresses or links contained in this book may have changed
since publication and may no longer be valid. The views expressed in this work are solely those of the author and do not
necessarily reflect the views of the publisher, and the publisher hereby disclaims any responsibility for them.

authorHOUSE®

This book is dedicated to the staff and students of
Ross Ford Elementary and in memory of Luc Fulton.
D.B.

Hi my name is Hunter and I want to tell you how I share my feelings. When I was five I wrote a book about the feelings in me. My book is called The Things In Me and one of the characters is my monster. I decided to have a whole book about them and how they affect my life. When my monsters are out I don't feel like doing anything. I don't want to play, eat, or even do anything fun. My monsters are not very good for me. The only way to get rid of them is to be aware that they are there and then choose them to be gone. The real trick is to know that you have the choice!

Thanks to my sister Piper for helping me learn these things about myself.
H.B.

THE MONSTER IN ME

By

Hunter & Darin Bullivant

Illustrations By

Mark Cromwell

Hunter, what came over you the other day when you wouldn't stop screaming at Grandma's house?

I got really angry and upset because I couldn't stay with Piper.

Can you give it a name?

I guess I would call it my monster. He was really big that day.

You mean he comes in different sizes?

Ya, sometimes he is big and sometimes he is small.

Sometimes there is a monster in me that comes out when my sister Piper takes something of mine. My voice gets growly and wrinkles happen between my eyes.

Sometimes there is a monster in me that comes out when I am tired or sick. This monster just wants to be left alone. When he comes out I curl up on the couch and act sad.

Sometimes there is a monster in me that comes out when I don't get to do what I want. This monster is really dark. He thinks dark thoughts, he has dark eyes and he even wants to break things or hurt people. This monster is even bigger because he scares me and I feel bad for thinking such bad things. He is an 8 on the scary scale.

Sometimes there is a huge monster that comes out when someone hits me or hurts me. This monster is very loud and sometimes I can't believe it's my voice that is screaming. I get a pressure in my head like my head is filling up with mad and it's going to explode. I have trouble talking and afterwards I am very tired. This is my biggest monster. He's a 10 on my scary scale.

Sometimes there is a monster that comes out in me when I don't tell the truth about my other monsters. Like the time when I hit Piper but I told Dad that I didn't. I felt sad inside and a bit scared because I thought I was going to get in trouble. This monster is kind of sneaky but he is smaller than the rest. He is a 2 on my scary scale.

There
are lots
of monsters
inside of me waiting
to come out. Sometimes
I let them out and sometimes
they come out on their own. The
secret is to notice that they are there
and then you can control them rather
than having them control you. Adults
call this being responsible. All I know
is that it's not much fun when my
monsters are out and I get to choose
to be free of them. The trick is to
know you have the choice.

Mark Cromwell
(Illustrator and Pretty Good Guy)

Mark was born very young. It was immediately apparent that he would develop into an artist of some sort. Now he is much older, as will happen, and he is still deciding every day exactly which sort of artist to be.

Upon receiving his BFA from the University of Calgary, Mark began freelancing as an illustrator for ad-agencies, restaurants and other clients. Approached by a client needing a caricature artist, Mark jumped at the opportunity and this grew to performance art of many types

His portfolios now include caricature, street chalk, commissioned paintings, and large-scale murals and installations for clients such as Bacardi Canada, Suncor Energy, The Calgary Stampede and Exhibition, Big Rock brewery and others.

Mark resides in Calgary Alberta with his lovely wife and three amazing kids who were all born very young as well.

A message from Hunters Dad.

Hi, my name is Darin and like my friend Mark I too was born very young. The cool part about that was that all I wanted to do when I was young was have fun. As I grew older I felt like there were things getting in the way of my having fun. As a student of Landmark Education and the teachings of Echart Tolle, I figured out what was getting in the way...it was things in me that, I myself, had created. When I figured that out I started having fun again. When I observed Hunter's behavior that day at Grandmas house, it was easy to see what was happening but hard to know how to deal with it. This book is about the conversation that occurred 2 days later. Hunter was able to understand her feelings, know that she wasn't wrong for feeling them, as well as create a plan for when that feeling comes up again. She is now responsible for what she creates and she is aware of what stops her from having fun. This has instilled the concepts of compassion, responsibility and love because the awareness of herself can then get transferred to others and she then understands we are all connected by this common thread. It is wonderful to have that connection with my daughter and the rest of the planet.

Enjoy our story,
Darin Bullivant.

Hunter's book inspired our family to live out our dreams as well as raise funds for several children facing life threatening illnesses. We have raised over $10,000 through the Children's Wish Foundation and will donate proceeds from the sale of this book as well. Visit www.daretodreamextreme.com to see our adventures or to donate directly to The Children's Wish.

CPSIA information can be obtained
at www.ICGtesting.com
Printed in the USA
LVIW020729030313
322281LV00001B

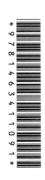